Picture the Past
Life in a Whaling Town

Sally Senzell Isaacs

Heinemann Library
Chicago, Illinois

© 2002 Reed Educational & Professional Publishing
Published by Heinemann Library,
an imprint of Reed Educational & Professional Publishing,
Chicago, IL
Customer Service 888-454-2279
Visit our website at www.heinemannlibrary.com

Produced for Heinemann Library by
   Bender Richardson White.
Editor: Lionel Bender
Designer and Media Conversion: Ben White
Picture Researcher: Cathy Stastny
Production Controller: Kim Richardson

06 05 04 03 02
10 9 8 7 6 5 4 3 2 1

Printed in Hong Kong

Library of Congress Cataloging-in-Publication Data.
Isaacs, Sally Senzell, 1950-
   Life in a whaling town / Sally Senzell Isaacs.
      p. cm. -- (Picture the past)
Includes bibliographical references and index.
   ISBN 1-58810-251-3 (hb. bdg.) ISBN 1-58810-416-8 (pbk.
bdg.)
   1. Whaling--New England--History--19th century--
Juvenile literature. 2. Seafaring life--New England--
History--19th century--Juvenile literature. 3. City and
town life--New England--History--19th century--Juvenile
literature. 4. New England--Social life and customs--19th
century--Juvenile literature. (1. Whaling--History--19th
century. 2. Seafaring life. 3. New England--Social life and
customs--19th century.) I. Title.
   SH383.2 .I82 2001
   639.2'8'0974--dc21
                                              2001000501

Special thanks to Mike Carpenter at Heinemann Library
for editorial and design guidance and direction.

Acknowledgments
The producers and publishers are grateful to the follow-
ing for permission to reproduce copyright material:
Corbis Images: Bettman Archive, page 28; Michael
Freeman, page 9; Lewis W. Hine, page 24; Robert
Holmes, pages 19, 30; The Mariner's Museum, New
Bedford, pages 8, 12; James Marshall, page 26. New
Bedford Whaling Museum, pages 6, 16, 18, 20, 22, 23.
North Wind Pictures: pages 1, 3, 11, 13, 14, 21, 25, 29.
Peter Newark's American Pictures: page 15.
Cover photograph: Peter Newarks's American Pictures.

Every effort has been made to contact copyright hold-
ers of any material reproduced in this book. Omissions
will be rectified in subsequent printings if notice is given
to the publisher.

Illustrations by James Field, page17; John James, pages
10, 27; Gerald Wood, page 7.
Map by Stefan Chabluk.
Cover make-up: Mike Pilley, Radius.

Note to the Reader
Some words are shown in bold, **like this**.
You can find out what they mean by
looking in the glossary.

ABOUT THIS BOOK

This book tells about daily life in the whaling towns of the state of Massachusetts from 1800 to 1860. During these years, whaling ships were familiar sights along the Atlantic Coast. Sailors on these ships killed whales and brought back their products. Whale oil was the most valuable. There was no electricity in those days. People burned whale oil for light.

Whaling ships also sailed from other states by the ocean, such as California, South Carolina, and Georgia. But during these years, many of the country's whaling ships left from Massachusetts. We have illustrated the book with paintings and drawings from the time, with modern photographs of the towns, and with artist's ideas of how whaling towns looked in the 1800s.

The Author

Sally Senzell Isaacs is a professional writer and editor of nonfiction books for children. She graduated from Indiana University, earning a B.S. degree in Education with majors in American History and Sociology. For some years, she was the Editorial Director of Reader's Digest Educational Division. Sally Senzell Isaacs lives in New Jersey with her husband and two children.

CONTENTS

Living By the Sea

A **seaport** is a town by the sea where ships stop to load and unload. Back in the early 1800s, many of these ships were whaling ships. They took whale hunters out into the sea. They returned to the seaports months or years later with whale products.

The whaling ships were important to everyone in the town. Many people helped to build the ships. Some made sails, ropes, and barrels. Others made clothes and food for the whale hunters to take on their long trips.

Look for these
The illustration of a whaling town boy and girl shows you the subject of each double-page story in the book.
   The picture of a **harpoon** and rope highlights boxes with interesting facts and figures about life in a whaling town.

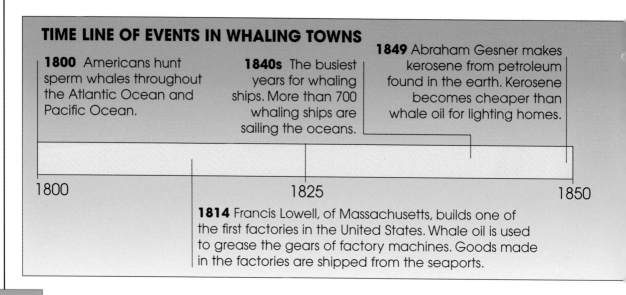

TIME LINE OF EVENTS IN WHALING TOWNS

1800 Americans hunt sperm whales throughout the Atlantic Ocean and Pacific Ocean.

1840s The busiest years for whaling ships. More than 700 whaling ships are sailing the oceans.

1849 Abraham Gesner makes kerosene from petroleum found in the earth. Kerosene becomes cheaper than whale oil for lighting homes.

1800   1825   1850

1814 Francis Lowell, of Massachusetts, builds one of the first factories in the United States. Whale oil is used to grease the gears of factory machines. Goods made in the factories are shipped from the seaports.

The main whaling seaports were in Nantucket and New Bedford, Massachusetts. In the 1600s, people could catch whales close to the shores. But by the 1800s, there were few whales left there. Whaling ships traveled as far as Australia, more than 10,000 miles (16,000 km) away.

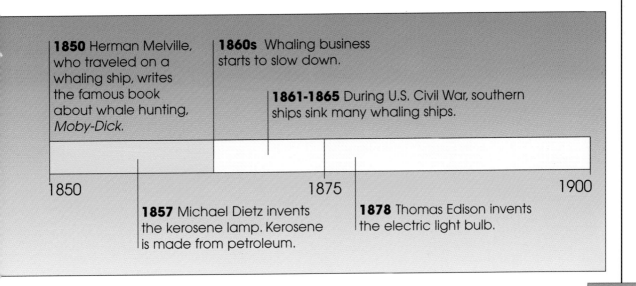

1850 Herman Melville, who traveled on a whaling ship, writes the famous book about whale hunting, *Moby-Dick*.

1860s Whaling business starts to slow down.

1861-1865 During U.S. Civil War, southern ships sink many whaling ships.

1850   1875   1900

1857 Michael Dietz invents the kerosene lamp. Kerosene is made from petroleum.

1878 Thomas Edison invents the electric light bulb.

A Busy Town

The sights and sounds of a whaling town were like no place else in the world. The day before a ship set sail was the busiest time of all. Clattering horses pulled wagons with tools and supplies. Chatty workers rolled barrels of food and drinking water onto the ship. Strong sailors dragged ropes and sails across the ship's wooden **deck.**

This is a picture of New Bedford, a whaling town in Massachusetts. The artist drew it in 1839. The tall white sails of whaling ships were familiar sights in every **seaport.**

The smell of salty water filled the air. So did the smell of hot tar and paint that workers used to repair the wooden ships. The businesses around the **dock** were busy, too. The baker was making bread. The doctor was stocking the ship's medicine chest. A clothing seller sold jackets and pants to the ship's **crew.**

LOADING, UNLOADING

Men that worked on the dock were known as longshoremen because they worked "along the shore." They loaded and unloaded sacks, barrels, and luggage by hand but used wooden cranes, hoists, and winches to lift heavy boxes and crates.

Long before airplanes were invented, ships carried people and goods across the oceans from one country to another. Today cars, computers, fruits, and vegetables still arrive by ship.

Why Hunt Whales?

A dead whale provides many useful products. The most important is oil. Whale oil is made from **blubber.** Blubber is the layer of fat below the whale's skin.

On a whaling ship of the 1800s, after the **crew** killed a whale, they cut up the body and boiled the blubber in large iron pots until it melted into oil. They stored the oil in wooden barrels.

Oil from this whale was used to light people's homes, to make soap and paint, and to grease the gears of trains and factory machines.

KINDS OF WHALES

Whale hunters caught many types of whales. Here are some of their names.
BALEEN WHALES
• blue whale
• gray whale
• right whale
• bowhead whale
• humpback whale

TOOTHED WHALES
• sperm whale

Spermaceti is another important part of a sperm whale. It is a waxy liquid found in the head of the animal. Candles were made from spermaceti. Ambergris came from the sperm whale's intestines. It was used to make perfume.

Umbrellas, corsets, and coils for chair seats were made from baleen, or whalebone, a tough, springy material from the mouth of baleen whales.

This is a whaling ship captain's logbook, pen, and scrimshaw from about 1860. A logbook is a record of a ship's voyage. The captain has shown the number of whales his ship had caught. On the sperm whale tooth, the captain has carved a message.

Jobs at the Seaport

Almost everyone's job had some connection to the whaling ships. The **cooper** made wooden barrels. The barrels held food at the beginning of the whaling trip. After the **crew** ate the food, they put whale oil into the empty barrels. The blacksmith made **harpoons** and **lances.** The crew used these to catch and kill the whales.

Barrels of whale oil were rolled off the ship. The cooper made sure that the barrels were sealed tight. No oil could leak out. He wrapped strips of wood or iron around a barrel to keep it together.

Three ships are being built on the shoreline. Workers used horses to haul heavy timbers to the wood-cutting yards. The ships had to be well built as storms and whales could break them.

Some people worked as ship builders and others sewed sails. Many people worked at the rope factory. A whaling ship needed thousands of feet of rope to lift the sails and catch the whales. Women worked in the homes and in stores and factories. Because so many men were sailing on ships, women ran most of the stores.

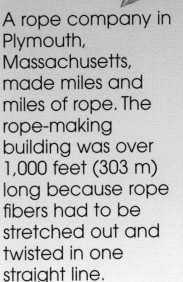

MAKING ROPE

A rope company in Plymouth, Massachusetts, made miles and miles of rope. The rope-making building was over 1,000 feet (303 m) long because rope fibers had to be stretched out and twisted in one straight line.

The Ship and Crew

Whaling ships stayed at sea for three or four years at a time. A ship had to be strong and sturdy. It carried three or four smaller whaleboats over its side. The **crew** used these to row closer to a whale in order to kill it. Sometimes there were more than twenty people in the ship's crew.

The sailors worked on the **deck** of the ship. They climbed up rope ladders to reach the sails. They slept below the deck in bunk beds. The captain and officers slept in cabins on the deck.

The captain was in charge of the ship. An assistant, called a steward, served meals to the captain. An officer was in charge of each whaleboat. There was also a cook, a blacksmith, and a **cooper.** A **cabin boy,** sometimes just twelve years old, ran errands and helped the crew. One of the most important jobs belonged to the men who threw the **harpoons** at the whale.

These sailors are boiling the **blubber.** The job is called "trying out." It is a dirty job, surrounded by black smelly smoke and sizzling oil.

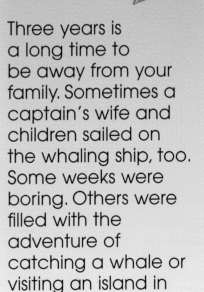

A FAMILY ABOARD

Three years is a long time to be away from your family. Sometimes a captain's wife and children sailed on the whaling ship, too. Some weeks were boring. Others were filled with the adventure of catching a whale or visiting an island in the Pacific Ocean.

Hunting the Whale

The **crew** took turns climbing up the ship's main mast to look for whales. Many boring weeks could pass with no whales in sight. But then someone would shout, "There Blows!" as a distant whale blew air out of its blowhole. The crew ran to the smaller whaleboats and lowered them into the water. With all their might, they rowed toward the whale.

A whaling ship's crew have rowed their whaleboats alongside a whale. Sailors at the front of the boats are ready to throw their **harpoons.** This is a **baleen** whale—you can see rows of baleen in the whale's mouth.

With any luck, the whaleboat got close enough for someone to throw a harpoon. Its jagged tip cut into the whale's body and stayed there. The harpoon was connected to the whaleboat by a long rope.

The boat pulled the whale. Then the whale pulled the boat. As the whale tired, the boat got close enough for someone to stab the whale with a **lance** and kill it. The tired men then rowed the dead whale to the ship.

FAR FROM HOME

Whaling ships stopped at **seaports** in Africa, Australia, Alaska, and Hawaii. The crew made repairs and bought food. Sometimes people from the distant places joined the crew. Sometimes the crew brought parrots or other pets aboard.

Whale hunting was a dangerous job. Sometimes the mighty whale tipped the whaleboat, tossing the crew into the sea.

Waiting at Home

While the captain and **crew** sailed the oceans, their families waited at home. Women kept very busy cooking, cleaning, and sewing. The sewing machine was a new invention, but houses still did not have refrigerators, washing machines, telephones, or electric lights.

Many ship captains lived in large houses. Some houses had a platform on the roof. Women stood on the platform to look for their husband's or son's ship sailing home.

COOKING: food was heated in a fireplace or on a wood-burning stove.
WASHING: clothes were soaked in a tub or barrel with soap and water.
USING TOILETS: people used a chamber pot and emptied it each morning or went outside to an outhouse.

While a ship's captain was at sea, his family celebrated birthdays and holidays at home.

Wives wrote letters to their husbands on the ships. Some letters took a year to be delivered. Some never arrived. Wives gave letters to men leaving for a new trip and hoped that the two ships would meet. On one island in the Pacific Ocean, someone made a mailbox out of a turtle shell. Sailors left letters there and picked up any that were addressed to them.

Around the Town

There were several stores in a whaling town. People bought bread and cakes at the bakery, meat at the butcher shop, and medicine at the drug store. Some men bought fancy suits from a tailor and women bought fancy dresses from a dressmaker. Still, most women sewed the family's clothes.

The "dry good store" was the place to buy everyday things such as flour, sugar, coffee, jarred fruits, candles, and cloth. It was also a good place to meet people and get the latest news.

In most whaling towns, as here in New Bedford, Massachusetts, some people lived near the stores. When they needed to buy something, they walked. Other people lived on farms that were farther from town. They traveled by horse and carriage.

This is a view of Mystic **Seaport,** Connecticut, as it looks today. In whaling times, horses and wagons would deliver barrels of nails to the hardware store and food to the dry goods store.

The **tavern** was a busy place. It was like a hotel, restaurant, and meeting place all in one. Travelers slept at the tavern. Sailors celebrated there when they returned from their trips. People of the town met at the tavern to talk about the town's problems.

A Child's Life

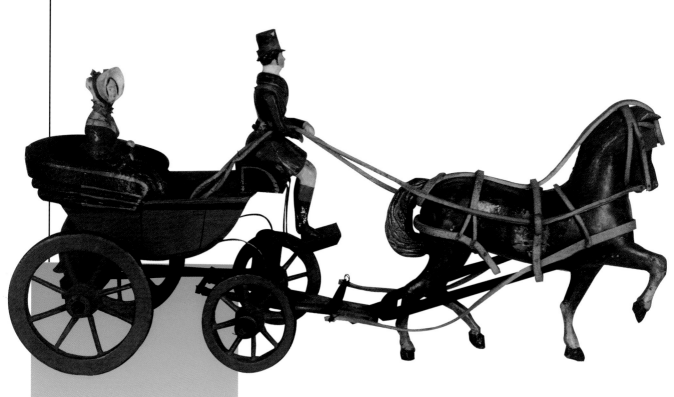

Children enjoyed toys with wheels, like this wooden horse and carriage. Firefighting wagons and trains were also favorite toys.

Children had many jobs around the house. They brought in wood for the fireplace. They helped wash clothes and hang them out to dry. Children also went to school.

Children played with simple games and toys. Parents liked children to learn while they played. For example, they gave their children a game of "Tiddlywinks" so they could practice writing numbers and arithmetic.

In warm weather, children enjoyed running races, spinning tops, and rolling hoops. The **cooper** gave them hoops from worn-out barrels.

A special treat was a trip to the theater to watch a "panorama." An artist painted pictures on a long roll of paper that was as high as today's movie screens. As workers turned the roll of paper, the audience watched an exciting story. A favorite story was "A Whaling Voyage Round the World."

GAMES THAT LAST

Do you know any of these games from the early 1800s?

- Pick-up Sticks
- Dominoes
- Tiddlywinks
- Marbles
- Old Maid
- Checkers

In the winter, children went sledding down snowy hills. Or, they ice skated on a frozen lake.

School

Before 1830, mostly rich families sent their children to school. Other families taught their children at home. In 1852, a Massachusetts law said that all children must attend school.

Students read from *The McGuffey Reader.* Every story taught a lesson about right and wrong. One story said, "Good boys do not play in a rude way, but take care not to hurt anyone. Bad boys lie and swear and steal."

LESSONS AT SEA

Children who traveled on the whaling ships learned about geography while sailing round the world. They learned everything about catching whales. Their mothers taught them to read and write.

This is a wooden school bench from 1834. Three students sat on this bench. Each one had a small table for writing.

This is a one-room school in Westport, Massachusetts, in 1815. Twelve-year-olds sat in the same room as eight-year-olds. The teacher talked to one group at a time.

Teachers wanted every student to read well, speak clearly, and write beautifully. Children also had lessons in arithmetic and geography. There was no place for joking in the classroom. Students who broke the rules had to stand in front of the class wearing a pointy dunce cap.

Clothes

Working clothes were comfortable and sturdy. Men wore long pants and shirts. On the ships, men needed waterproof boots and hats. They wore a short wool coat called a "monkey jacket." Women always wore long skirts or dresses. Girls always wore dresses, even to play outside.

This family lived in New Bedford, Massachusetts. These boys might join a ship's **crew** by the time they are fifteen years old.

When rich people went to parties, they wore fancy clothes. Under her dress, a woman wore a tight **corset** made of **baleen.** The corset made her waist look smaller. Over her corset, some women wore a "crinoline cage." It was a wire skirt made in the shape of a bell. The cage made the dress stand out at the bottom.

IRONING

Before electricity, people heated an iron in the fireplace or on the stove. They used the hot iron to smooth out wrinkles from their clothing.

These women are wearing corsets and crinoline cages. The wire crinoline cage became popular around 1857. Before that time, women wore many layers of dresses, or petticoats, under an outer dress.

Food

Most families grew their own vegetables in a field or garden by their house. They stored the vegetables in an underground room near the house. The room was called a "root cellar."

Fishing boats were always arriving at the **docks** with fresh fish, clams, crabs, and lobsters. The people of the town ate seafood in many of their meals.

Workers drop these wooden cages under water to catch lobsters. The lobsters enter the cage to get food. Once inside, they get caught in a net. The workers pull the cage out of the water with a rope.

Whaling Ship Recipe – Plum Duff

The **crew** of the ship ate mostly dried, salted pork, baked beans, dried fruits, and hard crackers. Sometimes the cook made this sweet dessert. A "duff" is a boiled or steamed pudding. Plum duff is made with raisins or prunes, which are dried plums.

WARNING: Do not cook anything unless there is an adult to help you. Always ask an adult to do the cooking on a hot stove.

YOU WIILL NEED
- 2 cups (480 g) flour
- 1/2 teaspoon baking soda
- 1 teaspoon cream of tartar
- pinch of salt
- 1 cup (240 g) raisins
- 3/4 cup (180 g) brown sugar
- 1 tablespoon vegetable oil
- 3/4 cup (180 ml) water
- molasses or maple syrup

FOLLOW THE STEPS

1. Fill a large pot half full of water. Heat the water until it boils.
2. Mix the flour, baking soda, cream of tartar, salt, brown sugar, and raisins.
3. To the flour mixture, add 3/4 cup water and 1 tablespoon oil.

4. Put flour on your hands. Then roll the dough into about 24 balls the size of ping-pong balls. (Add extra flour if the dough is too sticky.)
5. After the water in the pot boils, add the dough balls to the

pot. Turn down the heat to simmer. Cook for about one hour. Stir them occasionally.
6. Remove the dough balls from the pot and pour syrup or molasses over them.

The Ship Returns

Wives were never sure when their husbands' whaling ship might return. They knew the crew would stay out until all their barrels were full of whale oil. So the months and years passed. Finally, someone would spot white sails on the ocean. People ran to the **dock** to meet the captain and **crew.**

These ships have been unloaded. Workers rolled the oil barrels off each ship. The ship owner counted the barrels and paid the crew. The captain was paid the most. The **cabin boy** was paid the least.

The news of the ship traveled through the town quickly. By the time the ship stopped, the dock was crowded with happy people. Children hugged their fathers and older brothers. Wives cried to see their husbands and sons. There would be singing and dancing the rest of the day.

Workers will be busy getting the whaling ship ready for another trip. They will wash the **deck,** mend the sails, and paint the outside. In a few weeks, the ship will be ready for the sea again.

Whaling Towns Now

After 1860, whaling towns began to change. After so much hunting, there were fewer whales. Also, a scientist found a way to use petroleum, or oil found underground, for lighting. Then electricity and plastic replaced the uses of whale oil and **baleen.** Workers in the whaling towns found jobs in factories and other businesses.

The town of Mystic, Connecticut, has a museum-like village from the old whaling days. Many old ships are lined up at the **seaport.** Visitors can walk through stores and houses that look as they did in the 1800s.

Glossary

ambergris waxy material in a sperm whale's intestines used to make perfume

baleen tough, springy material, like human fingernails, from the mouth of baleen whales - also called whalebone

blubber layer of fat below a whale's skin

cabin boy usually the youngest worker on a ship who does chores for the crew, such as washing the floors, cleaning dishes, and serving the captain

cooper person who makes wooden barrels for storing and shipping things

corset women's underwear that fits tightly at the waist

crew people who work on a ship

deck top floor of a ship

dock platform by the water used to get on and off boats

harpoon spear with a steel tip, long wooden handle, and attached to a long rope, which is thrown or fired from a gun

lance steel spear used to kill a whale after it has been harpooned

seaport town by the ocean from which ships leave and return

scrimshaw works of art made by sailors from the teeth or baleen of whales

spermaceti waxy material in the head of a sperm whale used to make smokeless candles

tavern place where travelers eat, sleep, and meet

More Books to Read

Carrick, Carol. *Whaling Days.* New York: Houghton Mifflin Company, 1993.

McKissack, Patricia C. and Fredrick L. McKissack. *Black Hands, White Sails: The Story of African-American Whalers.* New York: Scholastic, Incorporated, 1999.

Index